THE ROAD TO THE ISLAND, AND BEYOND

BY

ADRIAN ROGERS

ISBN: 978-93-6354-574-8

First Edition: 2025
Rs. 200/-

Cyberwit.net
HIG 45 Kaushambi Kunj, Kalindipuram
Allahabad - 211011 (U.P.) India
http://www.cyberwit.net
Tel: +(91) 9415091004
E-mail: info@cyberwit.net

Printed at Repro India Limited.

Contents

PART 1—THE ROAD TO THE ISLAND

BY THE WAYSIDE–RESTING

I have unslung my pack
by the wayside
to breath-pause, rest,
looking ahead
along a grey road,
a self-goad
where half-dry grasses
in still green fields
test the road's edge,
and my mind yields
to unrestricted thought.

We brought nothing
into this world, and
we will take nothing
out of it.

Merely choosing to be
in this cattle-dotted land
scanning
a distant tree line
pine-dark green,
I have been
self-tuned, looking towards
a distant hill sweep
merging
on the edge of sight
into mountains.

ONWARD

Can the rose of time
blossom in the night?

I would leave a hard road
for soft sand,
directing my steps to an island
across blue green
foam/flecked sun/shot seas,
having and being
more…
than the sea wind.

A goad, like a siren voice
tells me—
to make a choice, putting
one foot before another.

Can a chime from the stars
turn darkness into light?

Athena—wisdom incarnate
dreams the island.
Revelation—herself
incarnating a light spark
elevates me
now and forever, but,
never by less than beauty's
eternality—truly a key.

ASH—A ROADSIDE MEDITATION

Along a road
under the light of day
I have stirred—in memory
the ashes of time
in a rhyme
interrupted, by what has
or might have been…

parsley, sage, rosemary,
and thyme,

but will not be again
in our time, until
a greater morning
dawns for a universe
whose inverse,
ash—is the last remnant
of organic life.

Ashes to ashes, dust to dust

until resurrection light
bursting, across
a dawn—white/gold/new/old
feeding an initiated
clarity of being
remembers time, as ash,
scattered to the winds.

PRESSING ON

The island
may not let me return
to lotus lands time forgotten.
What then, may I seek?

I have left highland, lowland,
green land ploughland,
journeying, voyaging
to illumination
from a world that is—
whatever it may seem to be
never enough.

Wildness…a voice calling
fades into the wind
as I look seaward.
The choice is—
to cross, or not to cross
blue/green wave-scapes
sun-flashing
as a black-sided curragh
rowed sturdily approaches
brushing gently
a shallow long-sanded
dune-grassed shoreline
on a whisper in the wind.

"Every step you take,
every voyage you make
is a line in the sand."

NIGHT ACROSS THE ROAD

The road, night-old
is stone cold,
and stars
blink/flash flickering
blooming
into darkness before
the rising of the moon.

Echoes—along a road
haunt me, old
in years like a tale told
merging
into voices bickering
footsteps padding
dark-across…bone hard
from a paving stone
bouncing back.

Moonrise—a wash
of white light,
again voices,
footsteps, hoof-beats,
choices—
to run, or not, when
'The Old Straight Track'
pulses—
star-moon glimmering
with the old magic.

ON THE ROAD—NIGHT WALKING

The night is…timing,
thinking,
listening, remembering,
footsteps
marching out, pacing,
rhyming,
hopes simmering.

Below a waking mind
good and evil
miming
tap on a dark road,
sharp/rap
on the door of conscience,
loading awareness
as night-breathed incense
goading
snaps into wakefulness.

A star-scape
shakes the soul,
moonrise white
floats a landscape,
nudges—
a mind awake,
takes a moon-star path,
shines a mystery.

THE ROAD—A SILENT DAWN

Sunrise, white/gold rising
above a distant mountain chain
dark-etched against the light
and the road a-shimmering

from east to west, glimmering
through forest, green pasture,
and sun-dancing water flowing
entwining green/gold vesture

is a song of earth and heaven,
'As above so below' enhancing
a splendor in time, glancing
across '*intimations of immortality.*'

For the seeing eye a remnant
of 'In the beginning' is captured,
a lightness of breezes blending
the whitest of lights enraptured
by the rose-gold of love.

How far…is the road's ending?
Will I catch a sea breeze flowing
in a moment's perception, maybe
a time of interception, glowing,

a bond unbreakable, a rhyme
for eternity, unshakeable,
'The Descent of the Dove?'

ON THE ROAD—THUNDER

I stepped into a luring dark
as dawn
broke the night apart,
skyscapes
hung black looming
cloud masses
drifting streaked to dart
their lightning flashing
scouring mark
from battlemented echoes,
claps...
crashes, sharp—whip-like
raps...
a rage of thunder gods
defying—
even the Archangel Michael
sounding
a judgment, trumpet-calling
centuries,
summoning the dead
to rise and look
beyond
time's elemental infusing,
defusing
false gods, out-ringing
a chain reaction of defiance.

ON THE ROAD—AN ELEGY

You passed easily into the sunset
and time became your friend.

Our road is oftentimes long
but circumstances bend,
perceptions distant are…light
visible at the road's end
and beyond, strong
to recall a greater dawning
light…invisible
until we reach life's seashore
gazing out
across the tidal waters of infinity.

You have passed onward into
that greater light
and after your passing, those left
remember…
catching the hemline of eternity
with love, yet not bereft
for we too will pass into the west
enduring its test,
casting off materiality and, like you

pass through The Gates of Sunset,
beyond time…even as a friend.

THE ROAD—A WAYSIDE VILLANELLE

The sun is blazing high overhead
pounding the road in a shimmering
beating down at midday's turning.

The road, a mirage is glimmering,
the heat, punishing is simmering,
beating down at midday's turning.

We are judged by the heat but not led,
by its dreams and desires never fed,
the sun is blazing high overhead.

I stop on a grass-hot verge, the urge
to desist is strong, tiring, a surge
beating down at midday's turning,

the grass underfoot, dry withering
intentions unsure and dithering.
The sun is blazing high overhead

yet...the river close by is a song
soothing, glittering, peaceful and strong.
The sun is blazing high overhead
beating down at midday's turning.

THE FOREST ROAD

A ribbon road
unrolls…
through a forest's
green gloaming,
a persistent, goading
awareness
when the bell tolls
long-light echoing across
a silence unfolding
as a presence looming
over…
a time/space mind-snap
unveiling without loss
a singularity.

Quietness the key
is temerity,
boldness 'to have
and be', but…in
heart-stopping stillness
a state
cross-shadowed by time
and a sounding-silence,
eternity
echoing in rhyme
a call—
to follow this forest road
to the island.

THE ROAD—BEFORE AND AFTER A SUNRISE

Night's diminuendos
are the arc-of-dawn's
up-lighting crescendos,

yet still…
as choiring voices
flicker-flit
through the fading dark
filling a waking,
shaking,
rending…of night's veil
slow-fast off-cast
into—a raising
splendored,
shadow-sweeping
dispersing
a new creation's gold/white
fantasia spreading,
but what…
of that sundering
silence, opening
on a green/gold whitening
shimmering?

Night's diminuendos
are the arc-of-dawn's
up-lit crescendos.

REFLECTING ON A SEA ROAD

The sea's voice in a shell
calls me…
to a pilgrimage of grace
renouncing evil
in time and place
hastening towards my goal,
being it,
waiting…on a bell-toll
shattering
a city's allure, lights,
deceiving
memories of loss,
unsure
since the world is dross
and confusion
to would-be-innocence,
yet the sea—
while time matters not
will be rising, until
evil, pounding on the door
is stopped.

Under a floor
of pinprick stars I walk
with angels, elementals,
one-pointed
towards the island.

ON THE ROAD—ANOTHER DAY'S END

Day's end, I pause,
shake off
the dust of the road
unburdening
a day's accumulated load,
my resting place
pre-figuring
the eternal caravanserai
of the soul,
and when jewel-bright stars
breath-pausing
grace immeasurably vast
night-black skies
my goal—
with absolute perception
is to try my inner hearing
on a night breeze calling me

…to perceive a divine nativity
in soft-night voices
prophesying
potentiality, mystery,
and recalling night
in a Chopin nocturne's
lucent-silver-toning
almost electrically haunting,

'Just the Way You Are'.

ON BECOMING A SEA ROAD

Sun flash and oars dip
catching the light
on a blue Atlantic swell
rising, falling,
wave-dancing, calling,
sun-sparked, stippling,
wave-sloped rolling
lightening a soul
as the Island, hazing
is a long-dark
horizon-wide dreaming
distance-perceived,
tested, imaging,

and a curragh lifts, drops,
oarsmen bending backs
to wind and sea
but the approach
seems unchanging,
cliffs dark, slopes green
stark to gentle
until a ranging mark
of jagged tops
edges softer pastures
glinting an emerald sheen,
as the boat nudges
a weed-green
half-broken jetty…

SPECULATION – THE JOURNEY

...but why have I travelled
through days
drought withered
on bitumen, gravel
and stones
making no concessions
to tired feet
attenuated bones
discarded possessions,
scattered memories
fleeting and fitful?

I travelled thus far
because this is a road
of saints and scholars
wandering, still haunting,
whose energy lingers
but not daunting.
I tread...
where they trod,
making my bed
in the smallest cell
hearing—if distantly
a saint's bell
and a chanted mystery
where the green sod
gives place...to stone.

TO THE ISLAND—AND THE ORATORY

I step…into silence
across a beachscape
of small dark stones
onto, a lip of grass
under a cloud drifting
…infinity,
where silence
is sanctuary, pulsating
gently into my bones
as the wind, subdued
is a singing heartfelt,
at peace
with memory's tones.

Birds seem silenced until
in a song-chant
calling, as I—
scanning a long green rise
into falling
perceive, by choice
a half-ruined oratory
of the soul…still,
in a valley opening
towards the sea
as birds, now choiring
echo back, to my vision…

"*Resurrect the Oratory*
for the Master's returning!"

RESURRECTING.

A wide/shallow green valley
opens westerly
towards an ocean illimitably
horizonless
in an afternoon's
red-to-gold slantwise sun,
where Time has begun
focusing…
on an oratory's grey-tones
between mild rolling slopes,
walls tumbling, roofless,
spirit-lonely,
infrangibly, intangibly
waiting…
for the Master—his curragh
long passed
below a vanishing horizon.

I am bonded to resurrecting
the Oratory
for the sun's eastward-rising
is destiny,
selfhood transcended,
heart and hand laboring
stone by stone,
in spirit, but not alone.

THE ISLAND—THE ORATORY RESURRECTED

Golden at dawn,
a high shimmering meridian
reddens toward sunset.

Light—has an infinite heart.

At night, shorn in part
of glamour yet held
by a mystery, the valley
is a cup of darkness
unspoiled, a time-dreaming
story…
and by virtue
of the '*Descent of the Dove*'
I will realize its vision
for light is '*darkness made visible*'.

Love, may be invisible
but is—in heart and soul
the reason for a bird's wing
catching the dawn,
salmon leaping
in a sheen of water-light,
a chariot of fire,
the Song of God,
Jacob's Ladder,
The Tracing Board of Love.

THE ROAD'S END—A DIVERSION?

I appear as a lightning-rod
at the end of the road
after endless miles
of dust and stones
under a burning sun,
yet…I am cliffs white,
broken, a goad
to climbers, my wiles
seeming unknowns
threatening zones
of uncertainty,
tempted by illusions
of power, confusions
perhaps…was I ever a light?

Deluded by strength,
walking, climbing,
stalking, my loaded ego
is on the edge
confronting a wedge
of possibilities
as gulls transmute
above the shoreline,
seen by love
as emanating, in spirit
the shrine's calling.

THE ROAD'S END—FACING WEST

In the dawn light,
a salt/weed tang
was breath caught
at the road's end,
as revelation rang
the Zend Avesta's
Zoroastrian perception
of a heart's goal
under the long bell toll
of time…
but the sea was a vista
fantasy-blue/green
wave-flecked white,
and the island
dark/green to purple,
sand-shore ringed
sheen-hazed,
elusive, but to me,
as one unfazed.
By the road's end
I will reach
the unreachable,
gliding into a light
where Time defers
to illumination, and I—
welcoming those I love,
pass on, into
light's consummation.

THE ISLAND—INTO THE WEST

Under a cloud-banked sky
I have left the green valley,
the oratory up/raised
for the Master's return.

Into the West I pass
over white-winged seas
on the call of wind, tide,
gull-flighted glissandi,
under a floor of stars,
hauntingly
yet undauntingly seeing
a curragh glide—
wave-rising dropping back
again rising,
for whomever I shall greet
in the far west
along the red shimmering
glimmering
spark-lightening track
of a setting sun.

Not mine the secretive test
of circulating time,
I know—
who will cross over
through shadow and on
into light beyond light.

THE ISLAND—CLOSING THE BOOK

I close the book
but lines slip out
as the fire burns low
though the ashes of doubt
glow—
pulsating with ambiguities.
I look—
beyond the last frontier
hesitating,
though I served with rhyme
and a chime
of radiance, resonating
beyond horizons
and showings.

Let it be so!
I nerved my arm,
strove for the right,
a greater, a burning light
by day and night.
Let the fire burn bright,
I have served my part,
The Master has returned
the Grail come home
and my people stand strong
at the end of days.

PART 2—BEYOND

THE PILGRIM'S WAY—A HARD ROAD

It is a hard road
jarred
by stones of illusion,
shadowed
by dis-illusion,
a time of self-reflection,
introspection,
defying rejection,
hearing responses
deflected, yet returning.

Rhyming is...coloring
trees and gardens,
whatever hardens
yet resolves, entangles,
untangles a mind
when a wind off the sea
caresses
memories of flowers
evolving
light's crossover refractions,
devolving, dissolving
awareness.
History may bide but...

who may abide
the day of His Coming?

THE PILGRIM'S WAY—A STONEY ROAD

The way ahead is a stony road
foot-rough
testing faith's endurance,
no bluff
but a measured tread
to a hoped-for goal at the last,
a resting place
for a lighter conscience
in a state of grace
where one may drink
from the spring, singing
Ave Maria from the heart
while the sun beats down
until sunset's frown
cloud-banding
bars the light—unless rain
flails beneath scouring skies,
but if love
fails not, as steadily we tread
in worn steps—
the living and dead about us,
grey towers
lifting and wide green lands
opening out
then we know that time's
eroding sands are stilled
...for a while.

THE PILGRIM'S WAY—WITH A FRIEND

"Friend, be a night wanderer,
soul-take
depth-darkness,
retrace old steps
towards healing, resolve
to turn
the ghosts of the past
towards their last rest.

Look...into the night sky,
fly—on the wings
of self-knowledge
smallest
in a star-spangled immensity.

Be...in worship
an intensity of knowing
before The Spring,
trending
towards holiness to sing
acceptance
of the blessing
on a star-studded path
to a fullness,
consecrating...this
moment
in a star-struck eternity."

THE PILGRIM'S WAY—LADY JULIAN'S TESTIMONY

I have visions,
but I say—
'Be...Thou my vision,'
Father,
Mother
revealed in a hazelnut,
'The All
within the All.'

I have not veiled my call
but testified
turning the nut in my hand
'That...all shall be well
and all manner of thing
shall be well.'

Healing,
I am healed.
Revealing
The Mysteries of Divine Love
I am sealed
with an eternal destiny.
A blessing
to solitary women
and cats
I fear not, walking alone.

I am custodian...of a mystery.

THE PILGRIM'S WAY—WILD SWANS

Wild swans wing-crossing light
overflying
a grey-towered shrine,
rising…
above green sunstruck pastures
in landscapes
synchronous
with enlightened searchers
time-distanced,
be renewing…
like a snowdrop's bloom
seasonal
though everlastingly the same.
Wild swans
of reed/haunted water-wild
light-flashing meres
dawn has begun her rising
and you—
hearing her wind-song,
or sensing
a sharp-edged storm
return—as matter transformed,
timeless,
transitional yet permanent,
close, distant,
as always haunted
but known…
by the magic of your name.

THE PILGRIM'S WAY—LENGTHENING SHADOWS

Green lands were quiet
under sun, and rain
around the shrine
yet shadows
crossed her light.

Shoes were left
at the Slipper Chapel
for a final walk
along well-worn paths
haunted by ages
pain-edged in stages
though with some
decrying our work,
but why did they hate us?

Minds were changing
rumors ranging
an age ending
but her 'light' was the same,
yet the 'Great'
invoked a name
in a febrile game
to shame old memories.

Shadows looming
crossed the light,
but we stood by Our Lady
at her shrine.

THE PILGRIM'S WAY—THE SLIPPER CHAPEL

I, am all I desire to lose
and walking far, choose
to heed an inner call,
leaving behind
my defenses
against, the reality
of a stony road
being—
where off-cast shoes
unbind—from senses
average sensibility
the self,
for one last mile
the verity,
as I seek to know
the asperity
of a disciplined love,
a temerity
outreaching infinity
where waits Our Lady
by the spring.

I, blessed by the waters
free from fear
sing in the changes,
Ave Maria.

THE PILGRIM'S WAY—THE SHRINE AND THE SPRING

My Lady deserves her shrine.

By a spring emerging
among trees and shrubs
we built her shrine
and pilgrims came—
the halt, the lame,
the blind and the kind,
seeking healing
by a power in the spring,
and the healed—by faith
were singing
My Lady's praises,
divine graces
perceived interspaces
between miracle, illusion,
order and confusion,
remembering,
miles travelled
despite hopes unraveled,
the roughness of roads
burdens, loads,
consciences, diseases,
with many healed,
sufferings annealed.

My Lady deserves her shrine.

THE PILGRIM'S WAY—VIGIL

To slip out of time
in the light fade
like an echoing chime
unmaking
the passing hours…is
a knowing
vigilant devotion
unceasing
as darkness, increasing
enhances love
expressing
in a candle flame
enlightened aloneness
tamed
by impulsive oneness,
like all…
who coming this way
to the Holy House
and the Spring
commune
in spirit with us today
tuning
their hearts to eternity,
finding
on their way, a fraternity
envisioned by love.

THE PILGRIM'S WAY—RETURN TO THE SHRINE

The way back
is an overgrown track
but also, an invitation
to stop, listen,
and hear Our Lady say…

"*Seek the sacred spring,*
drink of its waters,
let the heart sing."

"Let time take you back
past loss and breaking,
the shaking
of old foundations
to hear—
a secret rhyme,
see a shrine re-awakening,
a sacred spring cleared,
its promise—
enlightenment,
more than a token…"

So must a lark's song
be truer…than strong
delusions in our time,
truer, even
than memories we store
at heart's depth.

THE PILGRIM'S WAY—VILLANELLE OF LIGHT AND SHADOW

Among trees and shrubs there is a spring
where My Lady's form is a shadow
daylong across the light, a mystery,

a waltz of the flowers with fenland
grassland, and a pattern of ploughland
where My Lady's form is a shadow,

and the spring is a swift flowing tale
while the wind is a whisper, or flail
daylong across the light, a mystery

of harmony, counterpoint, story,
song, a shining, shimmering glory
where My Lady's form is a shadow

while memory is green as a song
first sung on a morning in spring, strong
daylong across the light, a mystery,

beauty, a bouquet of splendor, light,
shadow, remembered by day and night
where My Lady's form is a shadow
daylong across the light, a mystery.

THE PILGRIM'S WAY—LIGHTING A WAY AHEAD

Where now, Walsingham
in the backwash
of passing ages?

I turn the pages
of a convoluted history
seeking the twin branches
of a living mystery—
'Theotocus'
and the child,
but beyond the stages
of pilgrimage,
a shrine's ambience,
wild speculations
in a story's torn pages,
I focus—
on the Holy House
The Spring
their revelation as a glory
wedged
between roads trodden
by devotion
adoration—
despite loss, spoliation
and sorrow
to a dawn of resurrection.

PART 3—TIME/SEASONAL MEDITATIONS

LIVE PULSES—GOING DEEPER

Water over pale stones
is a sun-dancing glitter,
absolute clarity
but always a mystery.

I float above the bones
of an old world in a flitter
of perception, the verity
of a slow-dreamed story,

going deeper…

towards the dark
at the Lake's far end
where a long steep
forested, sloping
drop into depths
and mirrored trees
marks the Lake's edge
bordering—
unknown perhaps,
the hopes of some

going deeper…

where ancient pike lurk
torpid amid the murk
of their dreams, waiting?

LIVE PULSES—EASTER...

...descended from the stars,
could it be—
in rays or bars of light
outspread, a Southern Cross
or lyric haunting
Sweet-influencing Pleaides?

The Tree of Life
bearing all season's bounty
shapes, molds, verdant,
rife—with love's flowering
fruiting mystery
enflaming truth's knowing
timeless history.

What guides long years of toil
but innocence
and pilgrimage from nascence,
but righteousness?

So let it be—
a manifested illumination
up-lit across ages by Leo—
golden lion of a new risen sun,
wherein Easter
descending from the stars
blooms, in a garden's
time-endless resurrection.

LIVE PULSES—THE LARK AND THE QUESTION

A ring of light
and a lark soars
into the bright heart
of the day synchronous
with fire in the blood,
opportunity
in springtime flood
defying the importunity
of tradition,
yet. a day's first shadow
might be, specious,
a deception,
like that of the Greeks
besieging Troy
feigning a retreat, a ploy
to gain the prize,
a decision
historically inevitable,
conditionally predictable,
but listening
back through a year,
drawing near
to burnt and broken
memories, a token

countering fear,
a soul's bleak mid-winter
the long toll of war,
an abandoned goal.
…may there still be
a consecration?

LIVE PULSES—LAKE OF MYSTERY

I cannot see
into unplumbed depths
or be part of
a mysteriously
unknowable darkness.

Fish scales and fins
flash/flitter
in a blackness
of endless water-night
below
twilit worlds blue/green
shadowing.

Under the sun
a world-darkening
overhung
by a shadow/looming
tree/whispering
resonance
glides, into singing light,
a boat floating
on a dim-to-darker
mystery
of trees murmuring
their story,
is a consciousness
just touching…

LIVE PULSES—SONG OF THE HIGH HILLS

The hills, long-wide, high-rolling
leap…
into a bird-haunted, echoing,
steep-sided
sheltered green-lucent valley,
a sweep
of knowing dream-awake, close,
distant,
seamlessly perfected yet changing,
light—
across a sun-struck water flash,
a bright—
waterscape, a rushing light/liquid
splendour
catching a wanderer's gaze.

Grandeur…
numinous yet exemplified,
a singing wonder sky-wide calling,
rising, falling, tonally/wild,
swift light-shimmering,
glimmering,
sun-born, seeing, summoning,
returns—
beyond time. space, height, depth
…enflaming.

LIVE PULSES—RIVER NOCTURNE

My boat floats
detached from gravity
attached
to an interiority
of riverine/waking dreams,
themes
ripple-wafting,
whispering, blending into
a water-flowing
starshine glowing
before a moonrise
painting
a thin-pale light band
across
a minimally rippling state
released
from materiality.

Moonlight,
and a transitory…
shadow/water murmuring
elevates
and illuminates,
focused
yet suspended between
water/drifting
elemental forces
and a star-fire shining.

LIVE PULSES—CHANGELING

Autumn...a changeling
is sometimes
a spark-flashing
bright-water ring
under a black night
white-fired star-scape,
or sharp bright glories
of red-gold leaves
drifting...
under a morning sun
as if time had already
begun out-rounding
mortal existence,
defining
its temporary hauntings,
refining, or declining
existential hopes.

Who will remember—
one year from now
leaves floating
on a swift water-running
or a chanting
Autumn Wind's Requiem
for a summer's passing?

I will remember,
I am no changeling.

LIVE PULSES—A VOICE IN THE WILDERNESS

A voice echoes in the wilderness,
wild, unhinged,
a retriever of honey from the rock
sustained
by the locust bean,
his wilderness traced path
broken landscaped
for a son of priestly heritage,
rhymed heart-speech,
gleaned attention…

down/throwing the gauntlet
against darkness,
straightening crooked paths,
countering temptation.

A desert messenger
by power of water from the Jordan,
fire of purification,
an age's passing seen in the stars
he is…conscience,
prophetic timing,
heralding—
the Rose of Time, descending
into matter,
one who will shatter
presumptions of innocence.

LIVE PULSES—ADVENT, SPIRIT OF FIRE

A candle burns down
but the spirit of fire
is an endless advent.

St. John wears the crown
of winter, desire
in spring…presents
as fire of summer
spirit of prophecy
messenger of integrity
intense…
as fire itself, light, merit,
authority, summoner
unwilling to relent
or abandon his alchemy.

God-like in form
beyond the norm
of divine simplicity,
timed unstoppably
gendered into rhyme
he is…foretelling
the eternal expectation
of time as sacred,
focused, intending,
transcending materiality
yet becoming matter,
The Logos.

LIVE PULSES—TENEBRAE

Tenebrae—
of seven candles lit
only to be extinguished
one by one…

is no night-flit
but a self-examining vigil,
no flight from self
to a dawn beyond past
or present,
no escaping
until The Morning Star,
preceding
no elided challenges
gives place
before a newly risen sun
cantillating
Easter's morning splendour
into rising
over land and sea,
a perfect, tempered sign,
a new day,
a way, beyond time
…to be.

LIVE PULSES—VIGIL

Night in my cell—
within darkened walls
is chilled, my lamp
like a distant star
silently calling
audible from afar.
A dampened bell
is echoless for sleep
as visions creep
across hours and light
distances memory.
Hopes interacting
with hearts beating
hallow memories
flying, beset by joys,
sorrows, passions,
incipient experiences…

"Take him from camp"
…as one taken
by the living from
living a moment, until
moments held steadfast
are shaken. Beads click
through fingers slick
as a heartbeat's
decade soft/sounding,
but a beaded moment
seeded by night
is the finger of time
…until dawn.

LIVE PULSES—TONGUES OF FIRE

Darkness...expectation
firing, not cooled
by the dancing ring
of a bright fountain
is fear's encrypted
high-strung anticipation,
no silencing...for whom
the bells toll of any
whose gnostic vision
seeks a descending fire's
wind-rushing terrors
enflaming, purging errors,
spring-dancing desires,
rending the dark,
obliterating the mark
of Cain, emerging
into revelation's mastery
of time, space, place,
knowing, testifying,
...in tongues of fire.

So be it,
we—the knowers
accept no silencing
no dissolving
into ether.
We...are growers
of the future.

www.ingramcontent.com/pod-product-compliance
Ingram Content Group UK Ltd.
Pitfield, Milton Keynes, MK11 3LW, UK
UKHW041316190726
13845UKWH00025B/317

9 789363 545748